Editor-in-Chief
Sharon Coan, M.S. Ed.

Editorial Project Manager
Mara Ellen Guckian

Illustrators
Kevin Barnes
Blanca Apodaca
Alexandra Artigas

Cover Artist
Brenda DiAntonis

Art Coordinator
Kevin Barnes

Art Director
CJae Froshay

Imaging
Temo Parra
Rosa C. See

Product Manager
Phil Garcia

Publishers
Rachelle Cracchiolo, M.S. Ed.
Mary Dupuy Smith, M.S. Ed.

Puppet and Flannelboard Stories for Numbers, Shapes, and Colors

Authors

Belinda Dunnick Karge, Ph.D. and
Marian Meta Dunnick, M.S.

Teacher Created Materials, Inc.
6421 Industry Way
Westminster, CA 92683
www.teachercreated.com
ISBN-0-7439-3699-X
©2003 Teacher Created Materials, Inc.
Made in U.S.A.

Table of Contents

Introduction

Literacy is the key that unlocks all learning. Very young children can be introduced to literacy in a fun, playful way by using finger plays, flannelboard stories, and puppets. The variety of rhymes, poems, and literature selections provided in this series are research based and classroom tested. A variety of suggestions are presented to guarantee the use of standards-based curriculum to assist young learners in exploring basic concepts.

This book is one of three in a series that will introduce educators to ideas for enhancing language experiences, exploring creativity and imagination, and for teaching children to enjoy literacy. The materials were compiled to support teachers who may be pressured by the emphasis in education arenas to teach using standards-based criteria and the challenge of how to implement standards-based curriculum in a practical fashion in the classroom.

The Language Arts, Mathematics, and Science Standards for Early Childhood addressed in each section are listed in the beginning of the unit. One or more teaching tips to support the use of the materials accompanies each unit, as does an art activity for expansion of the concept. Ideas for supporting children with special needs, additional enrichment activities, and suggested books round out each unit of stories and patterns.

The activities included in this series are developmentally appropriate practices that support the whole child. The materials presented allow for kinesthetic (tactile), auditory, vocal, and visual stimulation. The mastery of oral language is a prerequisite to effective emergent literacy. Children learn about the relationship between spoken and written language as they hear, say, and retell stories. They begin to understand how to create a story sequence with a beginning, a middle, and an end. Children orally practice behaviors that will later be critical to learning to read (the link between pictures and words) and to write (the ability to say it, sequence it, and show it in print).

The suggested flannelboard stories and puppets are enticing visual and tactile aids that make learning a hands-on experience. By watching and then manipulating the puppets, children will solidify concepts while improving their motor skills. Puppets allow the young child a safe place to experience the world of imagination. Sometimes a shy child will speak to a puppet before speaking to an adult. Positive self-esteem is strengthened when children have the opportunity to successfully manipulate the puppet and tell the story themselves. The initial time spent creating these materials is well worth the effort, not to mention the fun! The patterns are versatile and can be used in different stories.

Each of the three readiness concepts—numbers, shapes, and colors—is presented in this book through a variety of literature selections. Simple, easy-to-make puppets and related activities accompany each presentation. Young learners are introduced to the world of mathematics and literacy by memorizing the different pieces of selected literature and acting them out with a teacher. Children learn to appreciate numbers and their uses. Additionally, number cards are introduced to reinforce the symbol/word association. They become aware of the different shapes, sizes, and spatial concepts by hearing and seeing these concepts presented in a variety of ways. Young learners begin to notice numbers, shapes, and colors in their environment. Later, they reinforce what they have learned by using the puppets to retell the stories amongst themselves.

The standards for Language Arts, Mathematics, and Science listed on pages 4–6 are met with the stories in *Puppets & Flannelboard Stories for Numbers, Shapes, and Colors*. These compilations of standards and objectives are similar to the ones required by your school district. The pages can be posted in the classroom for reference when planning lessons and for parent information. Family members are often surprised at the amount of "learning" inherent in storytelling.

Every attempt has been made to give credit to authors of individual stories, though many have been passed down through oral tradition. We apologize for any original sources we are unable to identify.

Standards for Language Arts

- ❑ Listens
- ❑ Comprehends what others are saying
- ❑ Asks and answers questions
- ❑ Demonstrates competency in speaking as a tool for learning
- ❑ Demonstrates competency in listening as a tool for learning
- ❑ Is developing fine motor skills
- ❑ Follows simple directions
- ❑ Identifies characters, settings, and important events
- ❑ Identifies and sorts common words into basic categories
- ❑ Produces meaningful linguistic sounds
- ❑ Produces rhyming words in response to an oral prompt
- ❑ Recites familiar stories and rhymes with patterns
- ❑ Recites short stories
- ❑ Recognizes colors
- ❑ Recognizes color words
- ❑ Recognizes meaningful words
- ❑ Responds to oral directions
- ❑ Responds to oral questions
- ❑ Retells familiar stories
- ❑ Tracks (auditorily) each word in a sentence
- ❑ Understands that printed material provides information
- ❑ Uses picture clues to aid comprehension
- ❑ Uses picture clues to make predictions about content

The standards above are a compilation from the National Association for the Education of Young Children, the National English Language Arts Standards for Public Schools, and the National Standards of English Language Arts.

Standards for Mathematics

- ❏ Conceptualizes one-to-one correspondence
- ❏ Divides objects into categories
- ❏ Classifies objects
- ❏ Compares whole numbers
- ❏ Connects math with the real world
- ❏ Connects math with other disciplines
- ❏ Copies and extends patterns
- ❏ Counts to 10
- ❏ Describes basic shapes
- ❏ Estimates quantities
- ❏ Explores activities involving chance
- ❏ Identifies equal/unequal portions
- ❏ Identifies shapes in the real world
- ❏ Identifies shapes in different positions
- ❏ Implements a problem-solving strategy
- ❏ Is learning number names
- ❏ Is learning number symbols
- ❏ Makes predictions
- ❏ Names basic shapes
- ❏ Recognizes and collects data
- ❏ Reads whole numbers to ten
- ❏ Solves simple equations
- ❏ Sorts basic shapes
- ❏ Uses verbal communication
- ❏ Uses pictorial communication
- ❏ Uses symbolic communication
- ❏ Understands the problem

The standards above are a compilation from the National Association for the Education of Young Children, the National Standards for English Language Arts, and the National Council for Teachers of Mathematics.

Standards for Science

❑ Applies problem-solving skills

❑ Classifies

❑ Communicates

❑ Discusses changes in seasons

❑ Explores insects

❑ Explores animals

❑ Explores reptiles

❑ Identifies body parts

❑ Identifies objects by color

❑ Identifies objects by properties

❑ Identifies objects by shape

❑ Identifies objects by size

❑ Identifies color in the real world

❑ Identifies the five senses

❑ Observes, identifies, and measures objects

❑ Predicts

❑ Problem-solves through group activities

❑ Recognizes opposites

The standards above are a compilation from the National Association for the Education of Young Children and the National Science Foundation (NSF).

The ABC's of Storytelling

Adapt the story for your group. Shorten, expand, or change wording for different age levels. The attention span of young children can vary tremendously.

Be creative with ways to enhance involvement and promote active participation. For example, ask everyone to clap when they hear a certain word.

Check for understanding, monitor and adjust learning as you watch, and listen to your students. Use children's names and tell children what they did. For example, "That is correct, Juan. You knew it was a blue square."

Devote time to preparation. Make certain you know the story and have all follow-up materials ready. Accentuate the plot and characters.

Emphasize the incidents that appeal to children. For example, the element of surprise can create vehicles for application in the real world. Use real-life examples and pictures when available.

Frequently ask children to respond. Ask them to repeat a line or give you a similar word. Plan ways to reinforce basic language principles.

Gain children's attention prior to beginning the story. For example, sing a favorite song everyday. The consistency and structure will help remind the children that it is time for storytime.

Hold the book so that the children can see, or point to, the figures on the flannelboard.

Individualize your instruction. Think about every child in your group and choose stories that align with their likes and interests.

Justify literacy! Send home notes to parents letting them know the book, story, or poem you are teaching. Ask them for support at home. Encourage parents to reread the story at home for reinforcement.

Knowledge of the early childhood standards will enhance your teaching. Review the chart provided in this book and integrate these standards into your lesson plans.

List the key concepts for a story, and repeat the learning throughout storytime. Make lesson planning a valuable component of your program. Keep the key learning lists and plan to spiral back to them to reinforce concepts.

Materials should be age appropriate. Use the teaching tips and expansion activities for children with special needs or those in need of enrichment.

The ABC's of Storytelling *(cont.)*

New books are wonderful, but the old favorites are just as grand! Use a variety of titles in your classroom.

Open, body, close should be the sequence of every storytime. Open with an attention-getter. Preview the activity, follow with the story body, and close with some type of review or follow-up activity.

Pacing is critical. Check yourself during the lesson: "Am I moving too quickly, too slowly?" If the children are restless, change the pace or try a different activity.

Question the children. Ask focused questions like "What else works like this?" Ask the children to repeat/retell the story. Ask, "How do you think the story will end?" Ask, "Do you know what will happen next?" Use eye contact and affirm the children's answers.

Repeat favorites; children learn through repetition. Reread or retell the story many, many times.

Sit in close proximity, at the level of the children whenever possible. Providing a set structure for circle time supports learning. Sit in the same place; always begin with a familiar opening, transition song, etc.

Treasure teachable moments. If a child wants to relate the story to his or her own life (maybe they have the same breed of animal as in the story), allow the time and use it as a teachable opportunity.

Utilize all available space, both in the area you are telling the story and on the board (if using a flannelboard).

Vary your facial expression and use your voice as a tool. You may want to whisper to emphasize a special part of the story.

Words you use should be clear and simple. Enunciate and speak slowly.

X-ray vision—Use eye contact as an antecedent to prevent unacceptable behavior.

Your attitude is contagious! If you have fun and enjoy storytime, so will the children with whom you work.

ZZZZZZZZZZZZ-end. Emphasize the end of the story and draw closure to the lesson with follow-up and/or extension activities. This will help children remember the story and concepts covered. And when they arrive home and a parent asks, "What did you learn in school today?", they are more likely to recall the story and concepts learned if there has been closure to the lesson.

Creating Flannelboards

There are many flannelboards on the market, however sometimes creating your own is more appealing. You know what size and shape your classroom can accommodate. Cut a large piece of corrugated cardboard to the size you wish to create a flannelboard. Cut a piece of felt one inch (2.54 cm) larger than the cardboard. Cover the cardboard with the felt, taping the overlap at the back. Note: Light blue felt makes a good background, since sky is often a good backdrop. Black, on the other hand, can be quite striking. Consider the following ideas when designing your own flannelboard.

Free-Standing/Tabletop Board

Easel Flannelboard

Pocket-Chart Flannelboard

Felt Apron

Creating Flannelboard Characters

Flannelboard characters are inexpensive to make and provide wonderful visuals for young learners. The patterns provided in this book can be made with felt or other materials and assembled together with standard glue or a glue gun. Some require simple sewing. All patterns can be enhanced with decorations. Use your imagination. Incorporate your own ideas and those of the children to construct personalized teaching tools for your own classroom.

Cut the original patterns out of heavy cardstock or cardboard and laminate them. These patterns should be saved in a central file area or in the same container as the figures and the story. This way, if one is lost or ruined it is simple to replace.

Tips for Enhancing Flannelboard Pieces

1. Use scissors with different edges when cutting out paper pieces to be attached to felt backing. Many styles are sold in craft, hobby, and fabric stores. Some have rounded edges, some are scalloped, and some have zigzag edges. Pinking shears are fun, too, and they work on fabric!

2. Keep leftover scraps of felt and fabric from other projects. You never know when a small piece will come in handy as a decoration, an eye, or a clothing detail.

3. Collect scraps of ribbon, bows, trim, and buttons.

4. Use leftover glitter and sequins for special details. Glitter glue and puff paints are handy as well. Consider using them when creating royal characters or when adding scales to a fish.

5. Yarn and curling ribbon make great hair.

6. Attach a small piece of Velcro® or felt to the back of most small puppets for use on the flannelboard.

7. Cut out characters from old storybooks and magazines. Attach them to felt with glue. Use these just as you would a felt piece.

Creating Puppets

There are many materials you can use to create puppets. Below you will find five different types of puppets and directions for their creation. Some will incorporate the patterns supplied in this book, and others can be made easily with household or classroom items.

Stick Puppets

Patterns for stick puppets can be copied onto heavy cardstock or cardboard, cut out, and decorated. Some teachers like to laminate the pieces. The cutouts can then be attached to craft sticks, tongue depressors, paint stirrers, or yardsticks for easy accessibility.

Mini stick puppets can be made by attaching stickers to craft sticks.

Don't forget about wooden spoons. Faces can be drawn or glued onto them to create almost instant puppets.

Note: When telling the story, whoever is designated to hold the puppet holds onto the item (type of stick) to which the pattern was attached.

Pop-Up Puppets

The element of surprise is a valuable attention-getting device in the early childhood classroom. Use a cylinder (paper tube), coffee can, Styrofoam cup, or paper cup for the base of the pop-up puppets.

Poke a hole in the center and insert a craft stick, sturdy straw, or dowel. Attach an old doll head (or a head created from a Styrofoam ball wrapped with yarn or covered with nylons) to the dowel.

Use a glue gun to attach the head to the dowel if the dowel cannot be pushed into the head. For added interest, decorate the hand-made head with yarn, fabric, etc.

Creating Puppets *(cont.)*

Hand Puppets

Use old gloves to create puppets for the number stories. Attach a small strip of Velcro® with a glue gun to each finger of the glove. Use the glove puppet when introducing counting stories like "Three Red Apples." Put one finger puppet on each glove finger.

There are many other objects that can be used for hand puppets. If you take some of the stuffing out of a stuffed animal, you will have a wonderful puppet. It is best to remove the stuffing from a slit in the back or the bottom of the animal. Leave the head, arms, and/or legs filled.

Mittens, paper bags, feather dusters, socks, a Slinky®, shirt sleeves, rubber gloves, and kitchen hot pads can all be used to create hand puppets. Use a variety of materials to create the face(s) of the character(s) in the story you are telling.

Face Puppets

Face puppets can be created on many household items. Consider using paper plates, dust pans, sponges, Ping-Pong paddles, fly swatters, paintbrushes, or wooden spoons. Decorate the faces to match the characters or animals in the corresponding story.

Keep a collection of face puppets to use with students to introduce new activities or concepts. Allow students opportunities to use the puppets to retell stories or to make up their own.

Finger Puppets

Simple, one-time-only, finger puppets can be made by covering a child's fingertips with masking tape or stickers. Faces can be drawn on the tape or plain stickers. Seasonal stickers, such as pumpkins, can also be used for specific stories or songs.

To make more permanent puppets, glue felt pieces or pictures to film canisters or cut off the fingers of old gloves and draw on them with a permanent marker or add felt details.

Finger puppets can also be made by cutting out two small, identical pattern pieces and gluing them together, leaving a small opening at the base for a finger to fit in. Any puppet small enough to fit on a glove will work for a finger puppet.

Additional Uses for Patterns

The patterns included in this book are quite versatile and simple to use. The more you work with them, the more uses you will discover for them.

- Reproduce the patterns on construction paper, and provide the children with materials to color, cut out, and glue the pieces together. Then, they can have a set of figures for each story to take home and practice with parents or other adults in the home.

- Use the patterns to create story mobiles and hang them from the ceiling.

- Magnetic strips can be glued to the backs of some flannel pieces for use on a magnetic board.

- Use the patterns as placeholders on the classroom calendar.

- Use the patterns to create an individual big book as a keepsake for each child in the class. For each book, cut two pieces of poster board to the desired size. Glue the pattern and a copy of the story onto each of the pages. Be sure to make an extra book for your reading corner or reading station!

- Children love to tell and retell stories. Consider making a second set of patterns for each story. The duplicate pieces can be kept in the children's story area. Allow children to mix and match the pieces to create new stories, or to retell variations of the favorites you have shared with them.

- Create matching games and/or sequencing activities using the patterns.

Additional Resources

Gould, Patti and Joyce Sullivan. *The Inclusive Early Childhood Classroom: Easy Ways to Adapt Learning Centers for ALL Children.* Gryphon House Publishers, 1999.

This book offers a variety of excellent strategies designed to adapt curriculum centers for children with special needs.

Sandall, Susan and Ilene Schwartz. *Building Blocks for Teaching Preschoolers with Special Needs.* Paul H. Brooks Publishing Company, 2002.

The authors provide many creative ideas for curriculum modifications, teaching and embedding learning opportunities, and child-focused instructional strategies.

Puppets and Flannelboard Sets

Artfelt, 1102 N. Brand Blvd., San Fernando, CA 91340 (818) 365-1021.
E-Mail: artfelt@mail.com

Artfelt offers a wide selection of products. Their quality finger and hand puppets are designed to also work on felt boards, bulletin boards, and pocket charts.

Ideas for Storage

There are many ways to store puppets and felt pieces. Try to keep all of the characters for one story in the same container. Always include a copy of the story. This organizational method can come in handy for people who do not memorize the stories and need the written words or prompts. Consider adding a list of the required props on the container. This is especially useful when some of the props used are from other stories or are materials used in other areas of the classroom.

Storage options include the following ideas:

Tape a file folder together on two sides and staple string to the top for a handle. Attach the story or write its title on the outside of the folder. List the props on the other side of the folder.

Label a gallon-size, plastic resealable bag with the title of the story. Enclose a copy of the story and the puppet pieces. Consider attaching a three-ring strip to each bag. The felt figures and the corresponding stories can then be stored in a large, three-ring binder for easy access.

Collect new pizza boxes (many shops will gladly donate them to schools). Attach the story to the lid and place the pieces inside. If you plan to stack these boxes, it is a good idea to label the side of the box as well.

Create a storage container out of a shoebox. Add a copy of the story. Laminate it if possible. List the contents of the box inside on top of the lid.

14

Numbers

Number sense is a critical building block to understanding mathematics. The information and poems on the following pages provide a gradual way to introduce each number individually. The poems are great fun to learn! Introduce the number poems in numerical order. Repeat the poem throughout the week. Reinforce the number the following week when the new number is introduced.

Teaching Tips

- When using puppets or flannelboard figures with young children, begin with fewer figures. For example, two little blackbirds (reinforce the number two). When the concept of two is understood by most of the children, add three, four, etc.

- The last poem in the number series is called Ten Subtraction Kites. For each kite shape, cut a strip (tail). Attach one to ten bow shapes to the strip for each kite. These are the kite tails. These felt kites and tails can be used to match colors, to count bows one to ten, and to clarify less and more.

- At the end of this unit there are ten number cards. These cards can be used for one-to-one correspondence and number recognition.

Art Activity

Photocopy the number cards on pages 46–49. Provide a copy of each number card to each child. Put several pie pans filled with shaving cream in the center of the art table. To color the shaving cream, mix several drops of food coloring into it. Give each child a paintbrush. Have them paint their number cards with the shaving cream.

Supporting Children with Special Needs

Repeat the poem "Review, One, Two, and Three" on page 17 daily. As new poems are introduced, continue to reinforce one, two and three. The goal is for your children with special needs to identify one, two, and three in a given length of time. Continue to program the child with special needs for success by identifying, holding, or replicating the numbers one, two and/or three as other numbers are introduced. Continue to teach additional numbers to the rest of the children.

Enrichment

Encourage children to create their own number poems. Write them out and teach them to the class.

Book Suggestions

Barber, Shirley. *Count with Me*. Five Mile Press, 1998.

McGrath, Barbara Barbieri. *The M&M's Chocolate Candies Counting Book*. Charlesbridge Publishing, Inc., 1998.

Toft, Kim Michelle and Allen Sheather. *One Less Fish*. Charlesbridge Publishing, Inc., 1998.

Meeting the Standards: Numbers Unit

Mathematics

- Conceptualizes one-to-one correspondence
- Compares whole numbers
- Connects math with the real world
- Connects math with other disciplines
- Counts to ten
- Divides objects into categories
- Estimates quantities
- Implements a problem-solving strategy
- Is learning number names
- Is learning number symbols
- Makes predictions
- Recognizes and collects data
- Reads whole numbers to ten
- Solves simple equations
- Uses verbal communication
- Uses pictorial communication
- Uses symbolic communication
- Understands the problem

Language Arts

- Demonstrates competency in speaking as a tool for learning
- Demonstrates competency in listening as a tool for learning
- Identifies and sorts common words into basic categories
- Listens
- Produces meaningful linguistic sounds
- Produces rhyming words in response to an oral prompt
- Recites familiar stories and rhymes with patterns
- Recites short stories
- Recognizes meaningful words
- Uses picture clues to aid comprehension
- Uses picture clues to make predictions about content

Science

- Applies problem-solving skills
- Classifies
- Discusses changes in seasons
- Explores animals
- Explores insects
- Explores reptiles
- Identifies objects by properties
- Identifies objects by shape
- Identifies objects by size
- Observes, identifies, and measures objects
- Predicts
- Problem solves through group activities

Review One, Two, and Three

One finger,
(Hold up your index finger.)

Two fingers,
(Hold up your index finger and middle finger.)

Now I have three.
(Hold up your first two fingers and the ring finger.)

Listen again and count them with me!

One, two, three.
(Use index finger from other hand and point to each finger as you say the number.)

Use the number pattern above and the patterns on page 18.

Patterns for
Review One, Two, and Three

Two Little Blackbirds

Two little blackbirds

(Sit down and hold up two blackbirds.)

Sitting on the hill

(Rest the birds on your knees.)

One named Jack,

(Show one blackbird.)

And the other named Jill.

(Show the other blackbird.)

Fly away, Jack.

(Move one blackbird behind your back.)

Fly away, Jill.

(Move second blackbird behind your back.)

Come back, Jack.

(Bring one blackbird back to the "hill" [knees].)

Come back, Jill.

(Bring the other blackbird back to the "hill.")

Two little blackbirds sitting on the hill.

. . . .

Use the pattern pieces on page 20 to create two little blackbirds.

1. Cut out two black felt bodies and two black felt wings.
2. Attach a wing to each body.
3. Add google eyes, an orange beak, and two orange feet.

. . . .

Patterns for Two Little Blackbirds

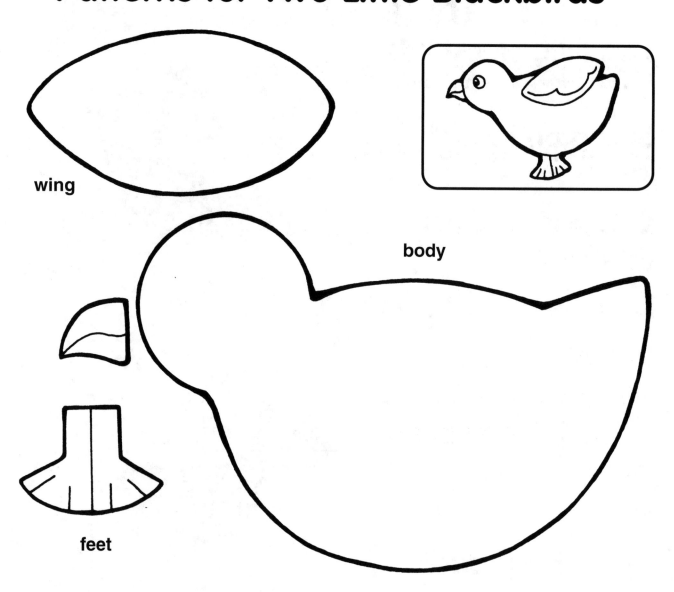

wing

body

feet

• •

Alternative Finger Puppet Patterns

Materials needed for each blackbird:

- 5" (13 cm) black felt square
- 2 cotton balls
- Small rubber band or black yarn
- yellow or orange felt for beak
- 2 google eyes

beak

Directions: Place the cotton balls in the center of the square. Wrap the black felt around the cotton balls to make the bird's head. Secure the balls inside the felt by placing the rubber band around the felt, forming a neck. Glue google eyes and a beak to the head of the bird.

• •

Three Red Apples

Way up high in the apple tree,

(Use index finger to point up.)

Three red apples smiled at me.

(Trace a smile on face with index finger.)

I shook the tree as hard as I could.

(Pretend to shake tree by forming two fists, placing them on top of each other and shaking.)

Down came the apples. MMMMMmmmmmmmm . . . were they good!

(Rub stomach.)

Use the patterns on page 22 to create the apple flannel pieces or the pattern below to create finger puppets.

1. Cut six 2" (5 cm) apples out of red felt.
2. Sew or glue two apples together along the outside edge, approximately 3/4 of the way.
3. Leave a one-and-one-half inch opening at the bottom for a finger to fit in.
4. Repeat the process for the remaining two pairs of apples.
5. Trim the apples with green felt stems and leaves.

Patterns for Three Red Apples

tree

leaf

trunk

apple

1. Make three red felt apples.
2. Attach three green felt stems to the apples.
3. Make one tree out of brown and green felt.

Four Fall Leaves

**Four little leaves in the fall breeze
tumbled and fluttered from the trees.**

(Place four felt leaves on flannelboard.)

**The first little leaf said,
"I am red.**

(Point to the red leaf.)

I shall rest on the flower bed."

**The second little leaf said,
"I am yellow.**

(Point to the yellow leaf.)

I'm a happy-go-lucky fellow!"

**The third little leaf said,
"I am green.**

(Point to the green leaf.)

**But, I assure you
I am not mean!"**

**The fourth little leaf said,
"I am brown.**

(Point to the brown leaf.)

I shall blow all over the town."

(Take brown leaf and whisk it across the air.)

- -

Use the leaf patterns located on page 24 to create the stick puppets or flannel pieces.
If you wish, make a large tree to place the leaves on while saying the poem.

- -

Patterns for Four Fall Leaves

leaf patterns

Make one red leaf, one yellow leaf, one green leaf, and one brown leaf.

Five Little Turtles

One little turtle, all alone and new.

(Place one little turtle on the flannelboard.)

Soon he finds another, then there are two.

(Add a second turtle.)

Two little turtles crawl down to the sea.

(Add the wave with one turtle hidden behind it, and move turtles towards it.)

Soon they find another and then there are three.

(Add a third turtle.)

Three little turtles crawl along the seashore.

(Add shells to the front of the wave. Move turtles along the edge of the wave.)

Soon they find another and then there are four.

(Add a fourth turtle.)

Four little turtles go for a dive.

(Place the four turtles on the wave.)

Along swims another and then there are five.

(Bring out the hidden turtle to join the other four.)

● ●

Use the patterns on pages 26-27 to make five little turtles, shells, and a wave. If room allows on your flannelboard, double the pattern of the wave to make it longer.

● ●

Patterns for Five Little Turtles

turtle shell

turtle body

· ·

1. Cut out five green turtles. Add google eyes if you wish.

2. Add lighter green shells to each turtle.

   Note: Reduce the patterns and apply Velcro® to the back of the felt pieces if you wish to use the turtles as finger puppets on a glove.

· ·

Patterns for Five Little Turtles *(cont.)*

shells

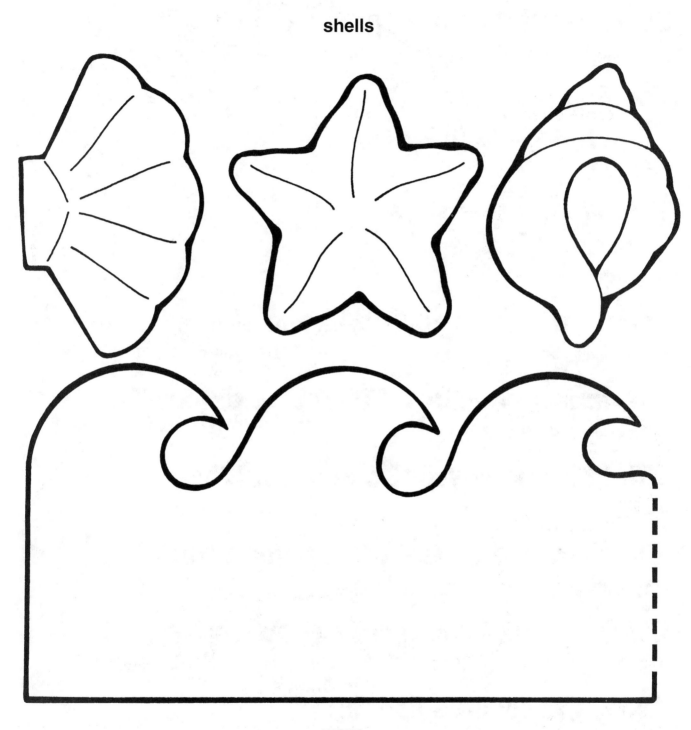

wave

1. Make two blue waves and connect them.

2. Make as many white, beige, or pink shells as needed to line the "beach."

Six Little Fish

Six little fish swimming in a pool.
(Count the six fish—one, two, three, four, five, six.)

The first one says,
"This pool is cool."
(Point to the first fish.)

The second one says,
"This pool is deep."
(Point to the second fish.)

The third one says, "I'd like to sleep."
(Point to the third fish.)

The fourth one says, "I'll dip and float."
(Point to the fourth fish.)

The fifth one says, "I see a boat."
(Point to the fifth fish.)

The sixth one says, "It's a fishing boat."
(Point to the sixth fish and add a fishing boat.)

CLAP . . . the fishing lines drop and
(Drop the "line" from the boat.)

Away the six little fish float!
(Count the six little fish as they float away—one, two, three, four, five, six!)

Use the patterns for the fish and the boat on page 29. If possible, use a piece of blue fabric to simulate the water.

Patterns for Six Little Fish

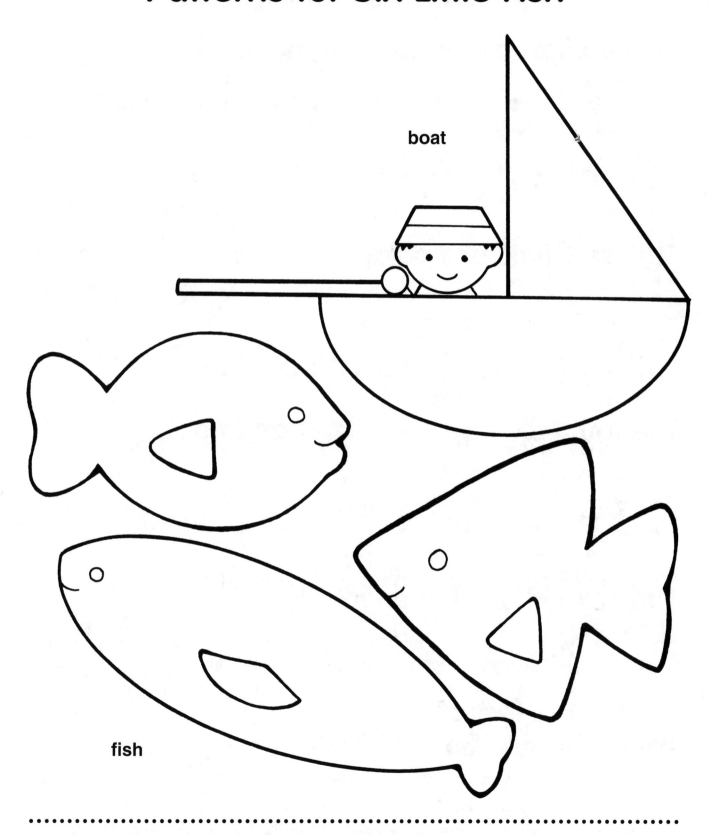

boat

fish

. . . .

1. Make six little fish. Add an eye to each fish.
2. Add a piece of yarn to the boat to suggest a fishing line.

. . . .

Seven Little Valentines

Seven little valentines were having a race.

The first little one was all covered with lace.

(Place the first valentine on the flannelboard.)

The second little one had a funny face.

(Place the second valentine on the flannelboard.)

The third little one said,
"I love you."

(Place the third valentine on the flannelboard.)

The fourth little one said, "I do, too."

(Place the fourth valentine on the flannelboard.)

The fifth little one said "My heart beats fast."

(Place the fifth valentine on the flannelboard.)

The sixth little one said, "I won't be last!"

(Place the sixth valentine on the flannelboard.)

The seventh little one was sly
as a fox.

(Place the seventh valentine on the flannelboard.)

He ran the fastest to
your valentine box.

(Hold up a decorated valentine box for children to see.)

1. Decorate a shoe box with valentine hearts to use as the box prop for this poem.
2. Use the patterns on page 31 to create the felt valentines.

Patterns for Seven Little Valentines

1. Make seven hearts. Each heart should be cut from red, pink, or white construction paper, felt, or other material.
2. Add lace to one of the hearts. Make one heart with a funny face.
3. Decorate each heart differently.

Eight Little Birds

One, two, three, four, five.

(Place the five little birds on the flannelboard.)

Five little birds flying in the sky
Said "hi" to the clouds as they passed by.

(Place the cloud on the flannelboard.)

And "hi" to an airplane and "hi" to the sun,

(Add both an airplane and the sun to the flannelboard and wave to the board as the birds say "hi" to the airplane and the sun.)

They love to flap their wings. Oh, what fun.

(Make a flapping motion by moving your arms up and down.)

Then swish went the wind and they all took a dive,

(Rub both hands together quickly.)

One, two, three, four, five.
Quickly, they landed in a robin's nest,

(Move the birds into the nest as the children count them. There should already by three small baby birds in the nest.)

Where three little baby birds were taking a rest.

(Point to the baby birds in the nest.)

When the wind calmed down and they decided to fly,
All eight flew very high in the sky.
Count them with me —
One, two, three, four, five, six, seven, eight.

(Point to each bird as you move it out of the nest and into the sky.)

Eight little birds flying in the sky.

Use the patterns on pages 33 and 34 to make the birds, nest, clouds, sun, and airplane.

Patterns for Eight Little Birds

small bird

large bird

nest

1. Make five large birds and three small birds.
2. Make one robin's nest using brown felt. Decorate with brown or beige yarn to simulate twigs.

Patterns for Eight Little Birds *(cont.)*

1. Make two white clouds and one yellow sun.
2. Make one airplane.

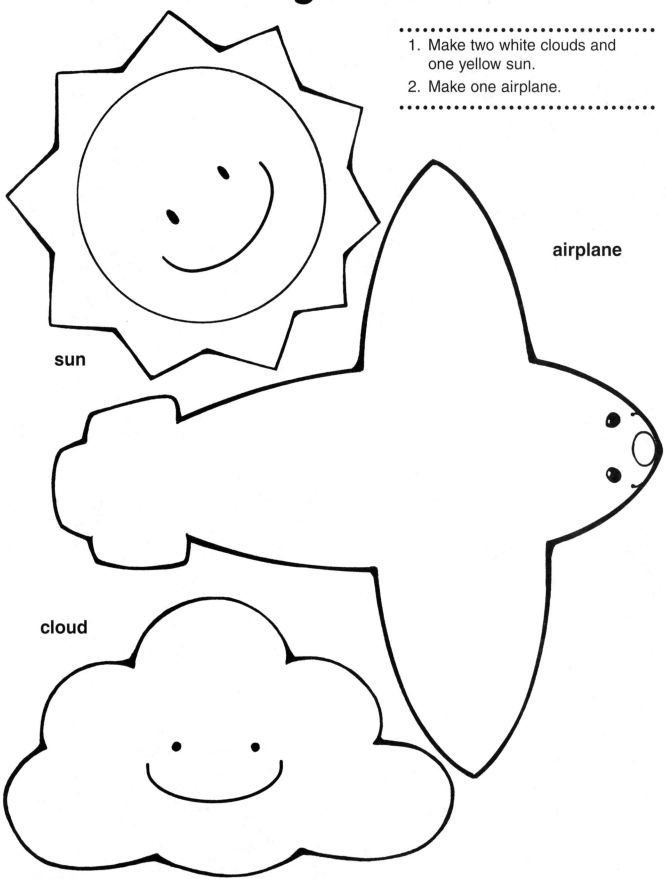

airplane

sun

cloud

Nine Little Ladybugs

One little ladybug
(Place one ladybug on the flannelboard.)

Ran out in the yard, out in the yard to play.
A fuzzy yellow duckling waddled by,
(Place a yellow duckling on the flannelboard.)

And the one little ladybug flew away.
(Move the ladybug off the flannelboard.)

Two little ladybugs
(Place two ladybugs on the flannelboard.)

Ran out in the yard, out in the yard to play.
A hungry red rooster came along,
(Place the red rooster on the flannelboard.)

And the two little ladybugs flew away.
(Move the ladybugs off the flannelboard.)

Three little ladybugs
(Place three ladybugs on the flannelboard.)

Ran out in the yard, out in the yard to play.
A baby white gosling looked at them,
(Place a white gosling on the flannelboard.)

And the three little ladybugs flew away.
(Move ladybugs off the flannelboard.)

Four little ladybugs
(Place four ladybugs on the flannelboard.)

Ran out in the yard, out in the yard to play.
A green frog hopped by,
(Place a green frog on the flannelboard.)

And the four little ladybugs flew away.
(Move the ladybugs off the flannelboard.)

Five little ladybugs
(Place five ladybugs on the flannelboard.)

Ran out in the yard, out in the yard to play.
A pink pig waddled by,
(Place a pink pig on the flannelboard.)

Nine Little Ladybugs *(cont.)*

And the five little ladybugs flew away.
(Move the ladybugs off the flannelboard.)

Six little ladybugs
(Place six ladybugs on the flannelboard.)

Ran out in the yard, out in the yard to play.
A black goat came along,
(Place a black goat on the flannelboard.)

And the six little ladybugs flew away.
(Move the ladybugs off the flannelboard.)

Seven little ladybugs
(Place seven ladybugs on the flannelboard.)

Ran out in the yard, out in the yard to play.
A white sheep said, "Baaaaaaahhhh,"
(Place a white sheep on the flannelboard.)

And the seven little ladybugs flew away.
(Move the ladybugs off the flannelboard.)

Eight little ladybugs
(Place eight ladybugs on the flannelboard.)

Ran out in the yard, out in the yard to play.
A gray bunny rabbit hopped by,
(Place a gray bunny rabbit on the flannelboard.)

And the eight little ladybugs flew away.
(Move the ladybugs off the flannelboard.)

Nine little ladybugs
(Place nine ladybugs on the flannelboard.)

Ran out in the yard, out in the yard to play.
A brown barking dog scared them,
(Place a brown dog on the flannelboard.)

And they all flew away!
(Move the ladybugs off the flannelboard.)

Use the patterns for "Nine Little Ladybugs" on pages 37 and 38.

Patterns for Nine Little Ladybugs

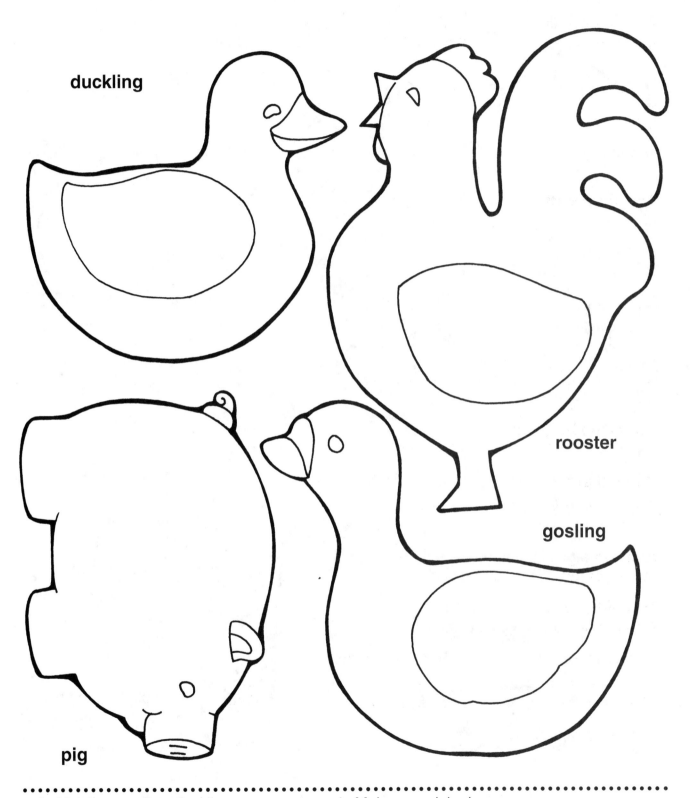

duckling

rooster

gosling

pig

1. Make one yellow duckling.

2. Make one red rooster.

3. Make one white gosling.

4. Make one pink pig.

5. Make one green frog using the pattern on page 89.

Patterns for Nine Little Ladybugs *(cont.)*

sheep

dog

bunny rabbit

goat

ladybug

1. Make nine red ladybugs.
2. Make one black goat.
3. Make one white sheep.

4. Make one gray bunny rabbit.
5. Make one brown barking dog.

Ten Balloons

Ten balloons I'll sell them to you.
(*Place ten balloons on the flannelboard.*)

White and pink, red and yellow, and green and blue,
An orange and a brown one, and a purple one, too,
And here is the black one.
(*Point to the balloon as you say the color.*)

I'll sell them to you.
Would you like to buy a balloon?
Let's count the balloons.
(*Point to the balloons as the children count them.*)

One, two, three, four, five,
six, seven, eight, nine, ten balloons.
Who will buy my white balloon?
(*Point to the white balloon.*)

As white as a ghost standing in line.
(*Take the white balloon away.*)

Now there are nine.
Who will buy my pink balloon?
(*Point to the pink balloon.*)

As pink as icing on a cake.
(*Take the pink balloon away.*)

Now there are eight.
Who will buy my blue balloon,
(*Point to the blue balloon.*)

As blue as the heaven?
(*Take the blue balloon away.*)

Now there are seven.
Who will buy my brown balloon,
(*Point to the brown balloon.*)

Brown as many sticks?
(*Take the brown balloon away.*)

Now there are six.

Ten Balloons *(cont.)*

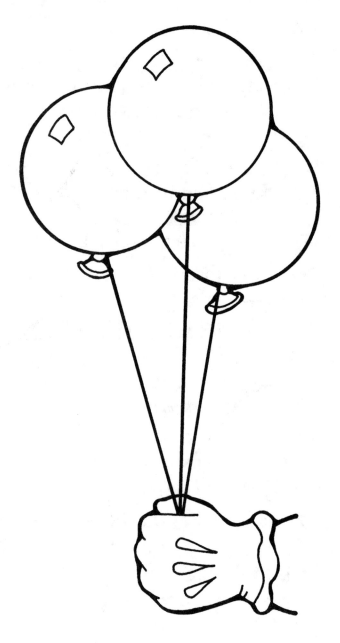

Who will buy my red balloon,
(Point to the red balloon.)

A color so alive.
(Take the red balloon away.)

Now there are five.
Who will buy my purple balloon?
There are not many more.
(Take purple balloon away.)

Now there are four.
Who will buy my green balloon,
(Point to the green balloon.)

As green as a tree?
(Take the green balloon away.)

Now there are three.
Who will buy my orange balloon?
(Point to the orange balloon.)

An orange is good for you.
(Take the orange balloon away.)

Now there are two.
Who will buy my yellow balloon,
(Point to the yellow balloon.)

As yellow as the sun?
(Take the yellow balloon away.)

Now there is one.
Who will buy my black balloon?
(Point to the black balloon.)

This one is just for fun.
(Take the black balloon away.)

· ·

Use the patterns on page 41 to make the clown and the balloons.

1. Make ten balloons in the following colors—white, pink, blue, brown, red, purple, green, orange, yellow, and black.

2. Cut ten strings six inches long and tie string to the bottom of each felt balloon.

3. Use the balloons with the clown pattern on page 41.

4. Arrange the balloons and the clown as shown on page 39.

· ·

Patterns for Ten Balloons

balloon

clown

Five Little Ducks

(Arrange five little ducks and Mother Duck on the flannelboard before commencing the story.)

Five little ducks went out to play
Over in the meadow and far away.
(Take the five little ducks off the flannelboard.)

Mother Duck said, "Quack, quack, quack."
Four little ducks came waddling back.
(Return four little ducks to the flannelboard.)

Four little ducks went out to play
Over in the meadow and far away.
(Take the four little ducks off the flannelboard.)

Mother Duck said, "Quack, quack, quack."
Three little ducks came waddling back.
(Return three little ducks to the flannelboard.)

Three little ducks went out to play
Over in the meadow and far away.
(Take the three little ducks off the flannelboard.)

Mother Duck said, "Quack, quack, quack."
Two little ducks came waddling back.
(Return two little ducks to the flannelboard.)

Two little ducks went out to play
Over in the meadow and far away.
(Take the two little ducks off the flannelboard.)

Mother Duck said, "Quack, quack, quack."
One little duck came waddling back.
(Return one little duck to the flannelboard.)

One little duck went swimming one day
Over the pond and far away.
Father Duck said, "Quack, quack, quack."
And five little ducks came swimming back!
(Place five ducks and Father Duck back on the flannelboard.)

Count them with me—One, two, three, four, five.
(Point to the ducks as you count them.)

• •

Use the patterns on page 43 to create the duck family.

• •

Patterns for Five Little Ducks

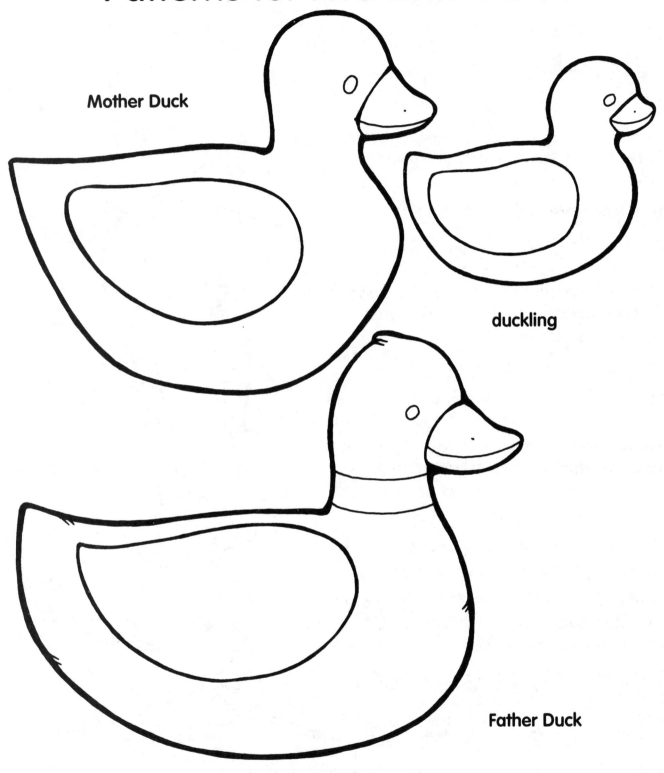

Mother Duck

duckling

Father Duck

....

1. Make one Mother Duck in gray and brown or beige and brown.
2. Make one Father Duck using brighter colors than those on the Mother Duck. Try a green head and a brown body.
3. Make five little yellow ducklings.

....

         #3699 Puppet & Flannelboard Stories

Ten Subtraction Kites

Ten little kites flying in a line.
(*Place ten kites in a line on the flannelboard.*)

One flew away, and then there were nine.
(*Take one kite off the flannelboard. Count the kites.*)

Nine little kites flying so straight.
Another flew away, now there are eight.
(*Take one kite off the flannelboard. Count the kites.*)

Eight little kites flying up to heaven.
One flew away, now there are seven.
(*Take one kite off the flannelboard. Count the kites.*)

Seven little kites flying straight as sticks.
One came down, now there are six.
(*Take one kite off the flannelboard. Count the kites.*)

Six little kites trying to dive.
One dived too far, now there are five.
(*Take one kite off the flannelboard. Count the kites.*)

Five little kites soar and soar.
One soared too high, now there are four.
(*Take one kite off the flannelboard. Count the kites.*)

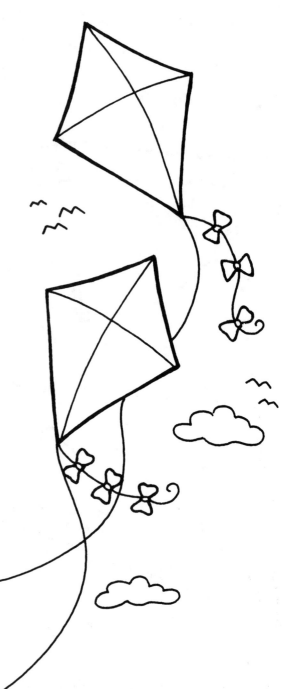

Four little kites flying over trees.
One got caught, now there are three.
(*Take one kite off the flannelboard. Count the kites.*)

Three little kites wondering what to do.
One flew away, now there are two.
(*Take one kite off the flannelboard. Count the kites.*)

Two little kites flying in the sun.
One got too hot, then there was one.
(*Take one kite off the flannelboard. Count the kites.*)

One little kite flying all alone.
(*Point to the one kite.*)

He got lonesome and decided to go home.
(*Take the last kite off the flannelboard.*)

No little kites flying through the air. Will they come back? Wait and see.
When the sun comes out and the north wind blows,
Maybe the kites will come again, who knows?

· ·

Use the patterns on page 45 to create ten kites. Each kite will need a piece of thick yarn or ribbon to serve as a tail. The appropriate number of bows can be added to each tail.

· ·

Patterns for Ten Subtraction Kites

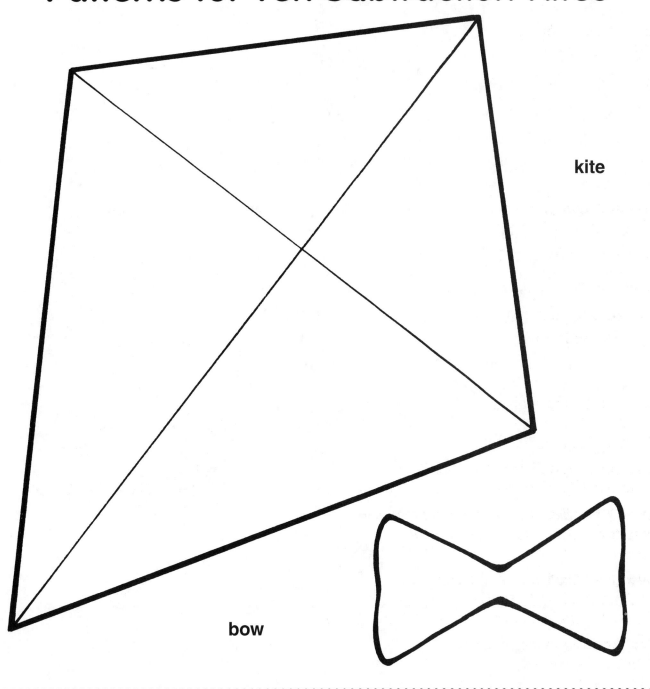

kite

bow

1. Cut six-inch kite shapes out of ten different-colored felt pieces.
2. Cut out enough bows to add to each tail. You may wish to add two or three bows to each tail. You can create a matching game for later by having a tail colored to match each kite.

Note: If you wish to add a different number of bows to each kite to go from one bow to ten bows, you will need 55 altogether.

The felt kites and tails can be used to match colors (kite and tail), to count from one to ten, to clarify less to more, and to practice basic math and subtraction skills.

Numeral Song

(Sing to the tune of "Skip to My Lou.")

Start at the top and come straight down (*repeat three times*)

To make the numeral **one.**

Halfway around and slide to the right (*repeat three times*)

To make the numeral **two.**

Halfway around and around again (*repeat three times*)

To make the numeral **three.**

Down, slide, and cut in half (*repeat three times*)

To make the numeral **four.**

Down, around, and put on his hat (*repeat three times*)

To make the numeral **five.**

Come right down and give it a curl (*repeat three times*)

To make the numeral **six.**

Slide to the right and then slant down (*repeat three times*)

To make the numeral **seven.**

Make an "s" and go right home (*repeat three times*)

To make the numeral **eight.**

Circle around and then straight down (*repeat three times*)

To make the numeral **nine.**

Make a "1" and add a "0" (*repeat three times*)

To make the numeral **ten.**

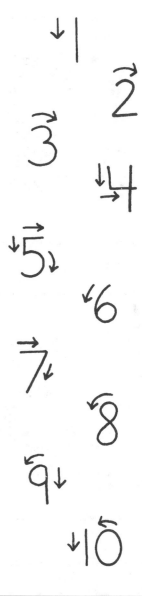

Number Card

Use the card above and the cards on pages 47–49 to enhance stories and reinforce concepts.

Number Cards *(cont.)*

2 two

3 three

4 four

Suggestion: Number correspondence can be reinforced during each story time by aligning the appropriate card to the numbers in the story.

Number Cards *(cont.)*

5 five

6 six

7 seven

··

Suggestion: Have each child match number cards as the various figures are counted at the end of each lesson.

··

Number Cards (cont.)

8 eight

9 nine

10 ten

Suggestion: Place Velcro® dots on the back of all number flannelboard characters and the matching cards. Play games to reinforce the one-to-one concept.

Shapes

Shapes allow children to understand the physical world. Children may explore properties of the various shapes by learning to sort them, seeing them in a variety of situations, and by creating their own shapes. Children will be introduced to the developmental language for shapes—square, circle, oval, rectangle, triangle, heart, diamond. They will learn the properties of shapes—curvy, spiral, corner, side, straight, zigzag, and discover how these symbols are represented in the real world.

Teaching Tips

- Help children to generalize their study of shapes. Show them how to observe the properties of shapes on the play yard or in the classroom.

  "Look, the tires are circles."

  "The end of the swing set looks like a triangle."

  "These storybooks are rectangles."

- Ask the children to create their own shape stories similar to the ones presented in this unit.

Art Activity

Provide shapes in different sizes cut out of cardboard, foam, or plastic sheets. Ask the children what shape they want to make. Help the children trace and cut out the chosen shapes on different colors of construction paper. Continue this process until each child has made a few shapes. Allow the children time to arrange the shapes on a large sheet of paper. Encourage them to try different patterns and arrangements before settling on a design. Then, give the children glue or paste to finish the project.

Supporting Children with Special Needs

Collect the variety of materials you have used to teach shapes and pick only one shape. Teach a lesson on the shape you choose.

Sample Script

"Remember when we read about Sandy Square, she had four sides to make her square. Count them with me: 1, 2, 3, 4. Look, there are also four sides on this shape. (Point to a square floor tile.) It is also a square." Continue until you have reviewed all square materials.

Enrichment

After reading "The Good Shape School" or "Shape Dancer," have children create their own stories using shapes.

Book Suggestions

Dotlich, Rebecca Kai. *What Is Square.* HarperCollins Children's Books, 1999.

Wilkes, Angela. *Colors, Shapes, Sizes, and Opposites Book.* Dorling Kindersley, 2001.

Meeting the Standards: Shapes Unit

Language Arts

- Asks and answers questions
- Demonstrates competency in listening as a tool for learning
- Follows simple directions
- Identifies and sorts common color words into basic categories
- Identifies and sorts common shape words into basic categories
- Listens and comprehends what others are saying
- Produces meaningful linguistic sounds
- Produces rhyming words in response to an oral prompt
- Recites familiar stories and rhymes with patterns
- Recites short stories
- Recognizes meaningful words
- Responds to oral directions
- Retells familiar stories
- Uses picture clues to aid comprehension
- Uses picture clues to make predictions about content

Mathematics

- Conceptualizes one-to-one correspondence
- Connects math with the real world
- Copies and extends patterns
- Describes and names basic shapes
- Divides objects into categories
- Identifies equal and unequal portions
- Identifies shapes in the real world
- Identifies shapes in different positions
- Makes predictions
- Sorts basic shapes
- Uses verbal communication
- Uses pictorial communication
- Uses symbolic communication

Science

- Applies problem-solving skills
- Classifies and predicts
- Identifies objects by properties
- Identifies objects by shape
- Identifies objects by size
- Observes, identifies, and measures objects
- Problem-solves through group activities

Shapes Song

(Sing to the tune of "Twinkle, Twinkle, Little Star.")

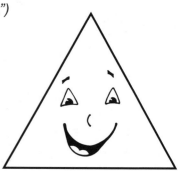

Tommy Triangle look at me.

(Hold up the Tommy Triangle puppet.)

Count my sides. There are three.

(Point to the three sides.)

Sandy Square—that's my name.

(Hold up Sandy Square puppet.)

I have four sides, all the same.

(Tap the four sides.)

Ricky Rectangle—I have four:

(Hold up Ricky Rectangle.)

Two long, two short, but no more.

(Tap the long sides, then tap the short sides.)

Cindy Circle—just one line.

(Hold up Cindy Circle.)

Make it round. That is fine.

(Trace around the edges.)

Use the shape patterns on pages 53–54.

52

Patterns for Shapes Song

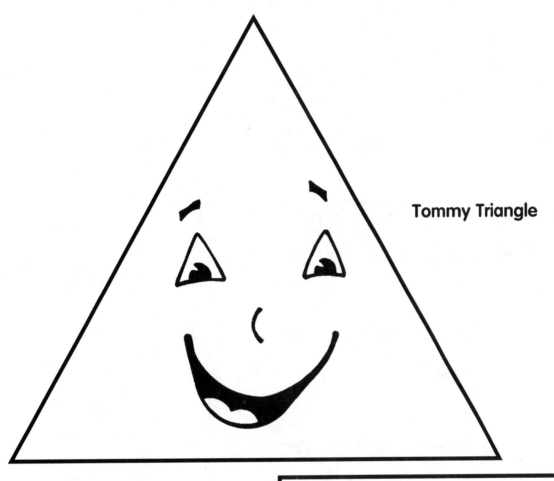

Tommy Triangle

Sandy Square

Patterns for Shapes Song *(cont.)*

Cindy Circle

**Ricky
Rectangle**

More Shapes

(Say aloud in the form of a chant.)

Sandy Square is the name.
My four sides are just the same.
Count one side and then count more.
Count 2, then 3, then 4.
(Hold up Sandy Square and count the sides as you say the chant.)

I'm Cindy Circle. Watch me bend—
Round and round from end to end.
(Hold up Cindy Circle.)

I'm a curved line that never ends.
(Trace the sides of Cindy Circle with your finger.)

Tommy Triangle is the name for me.
(Hold up Tommy Triangle.)

Tap my sides, one, two, three.
(Tap the sides of Tommy Triangle as you say the chant.)

Ricky Rectangle is my name. My four sides are not the same.
(Hold up Ricky Rectangle.)

Two are short and two are long.
Count my sides, come right along—one, two, three, four.
(Point to the sides as you say the chant.)

Danny Diamond is my name. I look just like a kite.
I'm really just a square, whose corners are pulled tight.
(Hold up Danny Diamond.)

Olive Oval is my name. My shape, now don't guess wrong.
I'm really just a circle, flattened and pulled long.
(Hold up Olive Oval.)

Helen Heart is my name.
My shape is the symbol for love.
(Hold up Helen Heart.)

I am a triangle with two circles above.
(Trace the invisible triangle and two circles with your fingers as you say the last line of the chant.)

Use the patterns on pages 53, 54, and 56 to create the flannel pieces or stick puppets.

Patterns for More Shapes

Danny Diamond

Olive Oval

Helen Heart

Shape Dancer

Shape Dancer, Shape Dancer, jump up high,

Shape Dancer, Shape Dancer, fly, fly fly.

Shape Dancer, Shape Dancer, bend down low,

Shape Dancer, Shape Dancer, there you go.

Shape Dancer, Shape Dancer, twirl around,

Shape Dancer, Shape Dancer, touch the ground.

Shape Dancer, Shape Dancer, hop, hop, hop,

Shape Dancer, Shape Dancer, now you stop!

Use the pattern pieces on pages 58 and 59 to create a marionette-type puppet. Have each child manipulate their own puppet as the class say the words to the poem.

Patterns for Shape Dancer

1. Make one large square for the body.
2. Make two small circles for hands.
3. Make two small rectangles for arms.
4. Make four small rectangles for legs.

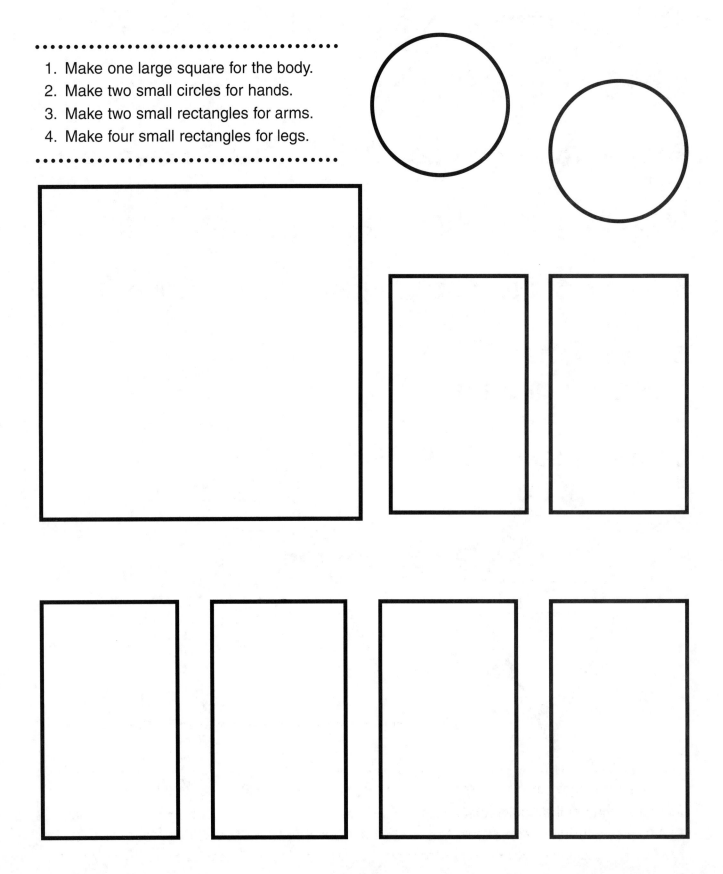

Patterns for Shape Dancer *(cont.)*

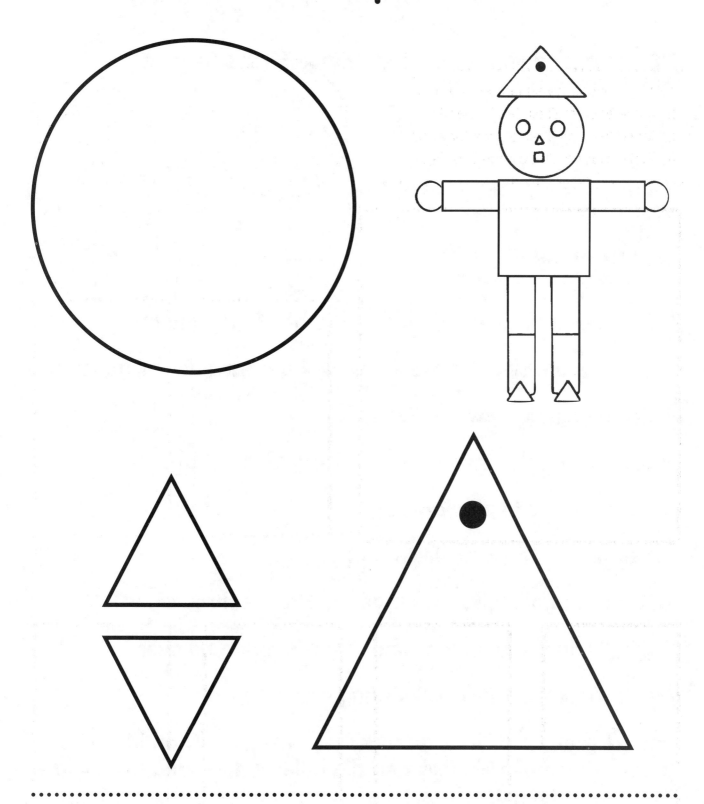

1. Make one large circle for the head. Add a face and hair.
2. Make two small triangles for feet.
3. Make one medium-size brown triangle. Punch a hole in the top to add a string.

The Good Shape School

by Christy Griffin

Hi, we're glad you came to The Good Shape School.
(Put up schoolhouse.)

This is Miss Morningstar. She's the teacher.
(Put up star figure.)

There are six children in her class.
(Add six shapes.)

Let's meet them.
(Point to each as you talk about them.)

Darcy Diamond likes to dance. She has four corners.

Sandy Square sings all the time. He has four sides all the same.

Ricky Rectangle runs and hides.

He has four sides; two are long and two are short.

Ollie Oval likes to play outside.

When he rolls he looks like an egg.

Tommy Triangle talks to everyone. He has three sides.

Cindy Circle is ready for school. She is round all over.

Miss Morningstar makes learning lots of fun.

The children do everything together. They climb and they paint. They build big hills and dig holes in the sandbox. And they like to look at books.

One day Sandy, Ricky, Tommy, and Darcy told Ollie and Cindy that they did not want to be their friends.

The Good Shape School *(cont.)*

They said, "We don't like you! You're different from us."

Cindy and Ollie were sad and asked, "Why are we different?"

"You are curved and have no corners, that's why!"
said the other four children.

Miss Morningstar listened to the problem and told the children,
"It does not matter what you look like on the outside.
We're all the same on the inside."

"What do you mean?" they said.

"We may look different on the outside, but we all have the
same shape inside, and that's what counts,"
said Miss Morningstar.

"What shape is that?" they asked.

"A heart. Hearts have corners and curves."
And sure enough, all the children had a heart,
even Miss Morningstar.
(Turn the puppets over and show the children the hearts.)

That's what made them all alike,
and they were friends again.

They were happy at The Good Shape School and that made
Miss Morningstar happy too.

. . . .

1. Recreate the set of shape puppets from pages 53, 54, and 56.
2. Make the puppets on page 62.
3. Glue a red felt heart on the back of each of the shape pieces.

. . . .

Patterns for The Good Shape School

1. Make one Miss Morningstar. Add a red heart to the back.

2. Make one schoolhouse.

3. Make seven red felt hearts.

Five Busy Shapes

Four squares and three circles went out to play.
(Put four squares and three circles on the flannelboard.)

Since circles are round, they rolled away.
(Turn the circles in a round rolling motion as you take them off the board.)

With four equal sides, all straight and all flat,
(Point to the four sides.)

The squares couldn't roll; so they just sat.

Two squares were quite big; two were really small,
(Point to the large squares and then the small ones.)

But that didn't bother the small squares at all.

One little square said to the other,

"We're exactly alike, so let's get together."
(Point to the two small squares.)

Pressed side by side in sort of a tangle,

The two alike squares made a rectangle.
(Put the two squares together on top of the rectangle.)

Then two little circles that weren't far apart,

Rolled up to the rectangle to help make a cart.
(Put circles under the rectangle to look like wheels.)

The cart was so cute and cozy inside;

In jumped a mouse and went for a ride.
(Place the mouse on top of the rectangle.)

"If I had a roof, I'd make a house,"

Said Big Square One, "A house for the mouse."

"I'll make the roof," said Big Square Two.

Five Busy Shapes (cont.)

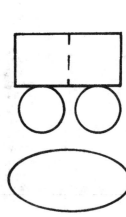

"Cut me in half and I'll show you."

From corner to corner, cut straight through.

That square made a triangle; in fact, he made two.

(Show how the square becomes two triangles by slowly pulling the two apart.)

He made one for a roof to shelter the mouse

(Put one triangle just above the big square.)

And one for a tree to plant by the house.

(Put one triangle on its side, with a point down next to the house.)

When the mouse-house was built, in less
than a minute, that mouse parked his cart
and began living in it.

The third busy circle they didn't forget;

They just hadn't found a good use for him yet.

"Oh, look," said Third Circle as he squeezed
himself flat, "Now I'm an oval.

Wow, look at that!"

(Exchange the oval for the circle.)

"Out by the house I'll make a pool,

Where Mouse can go swimming and keep nice and cool."

When the pool was all finished, the mouse they called Jim

Ran out of the house and went for a swim.

(Move mouse into the pool.)

Now Jim had a house, a cart, and a tree,

And a pool to keep cool, and
all of them free!

Make the patterns on pages 65–66.

Patterns for Five Busy Shapes

1. Make one large blue oval.
2. Make one large red square.
3. Make two medium yellow squares.
4. Make one mouse.

Patterns for Five Busy Shapes (cont.)

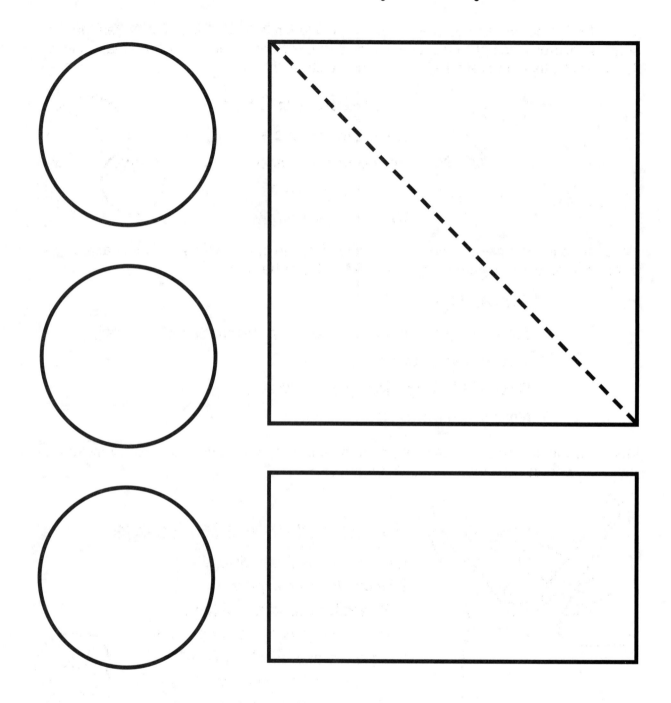

1. Make three medium blue circles.
2. Make one large green rectangle.
3. Make a large green square and cut it to form two triangles.

Circle Time

The following poems can be presented during the circle time. Circles are often the first shapes children attempt to make. Research in early childhood has shown that a circle is also the most challenging basic shape for young children to learn.

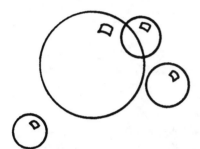

Round in the Circle

Round in the circle

Round in the game

Round in the circle

What's your name?

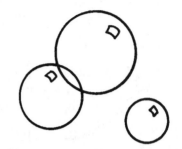

Have students hold hands and form a circle. Say the above words and ask each student his or her name. Each can shout it out when it is his or her turn.

Stand Up

Stand up (child's name), stand up (repeat child's name),

Turn around, turn around,

Give a little clap clap, give a little clap.

Now sit down, now sit down.

Model for the children first, saying the chant and using your own name. They move around the room and use a variety of student names.

Round and Round the Village

Let's fly around the village.

(Pretend to be an airplane.)

Let's walk around the village.

(Also use jump, hop, skip, or gallop.)

Let's drive around the village.

(Pretend to be driving a car.)

Let's swim around the pool.

(Pretend to swim.)

Let's row around the lake.

(Pretend to row a boat.)

Let's paddle down the river.

(Pretend to paddle a canoe.)

Let's . . .

(Get ideas from students.)

Colors

Children learn basic colors by association (green frog, blue sky). The poems in this unit reinforce these associations. The suggested activities support the hypothesis that experimenting with primary colors (*red, blue, yellow*) allows a child to discover the scientific wonder of secondary combinations (*purple, green, orange*). Children can be introduced to colors at a very young age. Recognizing colors can develop as late as five years of age.

Teaching Tips

Children learn colors through exploration. Set up a color center where children can explore color using prisms, kaleidoscopes, clear transparent plastic pieces, color paddles, etc. In day-to-day activities use color descriptions. Mention the "blue sky" or "green trees."

Help children discover the properties of colors by putting two primary colors at the painting easels at a time. Blending the two primary colors will create secondary colors. **Note:** If you put out all three colors during initial explorations, you may end up with brown!

Art Activity

Land of Red: Set up several tables for finger painting, with finger-painting paper and a different colored paint at each table. Tell the following story:

> *Once there was a Land of Red, where everything was red. The sky was red, the grass was red, the trees and animals were red, and even the people were red. But if anyone got tired of seeing red, that person just needed to look over the red hills to the Land of Yellow, where everything was yellow. The sky was yellow, the grass was yellow, the trees and animals were yellow, and even the water was yellow. But just over the hills was the Land of Blue. (Continue with other colors.)*

Ask the children which land they like best. Have them go to the table with that color paint, and paint a picture of the land they imagine.

Supporting Children with Special Needs

Enhance fine motor skills with this eye-hand coordination activity. Provide each child with a white plastic ice cube tray. Put red, yellow, and blue colored water in three of the cube holders. Encourage the child to experiment using a plastic eyedropper to blend drops of colored water to make a new color. If the child is not capable of manipulating eyedroppers, dip cotton balls into the colored water instead. Later, have children drop colored water onto white coffee filters. (Suggestion: Start with two colors, red and yellow or red and blue or yellow and blue. Each will make a secondary color.) Your students will be excited to see the "color magic!")

Enrichment

Magic Color Toast: Gather white bread, milk, food coloring, bowls, unused small paintbrushes, a toaster oven, and butter or honey (optional).

Pour milk into three or more small bowls. Add a different color of food color to each bowl. Stir. Paint designs onto bread with the colored milk. Toast the bread. Eat and enjoy.

Book Suggestions

Carle, Eric. *Brown Bear, Brown Bear, What Do You See?* Henry Holt and Company, 1996.
Hubbard, Patricia. *My Crayons Talk.* Henry Holt and Company, 1999.

Meeting the Standards: Colors Unit

Language Arts

- Comprehends what others are saying
- Demonstrates competency in speaking as a tool for learning
- Demonstrates competency in listening as a tool for learning
- Is developing fine motor skills
- Follows simple directions
- Identifies characters, settings, and important events
- Identifies and sorts common words into basic categories
- Produces meaningful linguistic sounds
- Produces rhyming words in response to an oral prompt
- Recognizes colors
- Recognizes color words
- Recognizes meaningful words
- Responds to oral directions
- Responds to oral questions
- Retells familiar stories
- Tracks (auditorily) each word in a sentence
- Understands that printed material provides information
- Uses picture clues to aid comprehension
- Uses picture clues to make predictions about content

Mathematics

- Conceptualizes one-to-one correspondence
- Divides objects into categories
- Classifies objects
- Explores activities involving chance
- Names basic shapes
- Recognizes and collects data
- Uses verbal communication
- Uses pictorial communication
- Uses symbolic communication

Science

- Applies problem-solving skills
- Classifies
- Communicates
- Explores animals
- Identifies body parts
- Identifies the five senses
- Identifies objects by color
- Identifies objects by properties
- Identifies objects by shape
- Identifies objects by size
- Identifies color in the real world

Little White Duck

There's a little white duck, sitting in the water.
(*Put the pond, the duck, and the lily pad on the flannelboard.*)

A little white duck, doing what he oughta!
He took a bite of the lily pad,
Flapped his wings, and he said, "I'm glad
I'm a little white duck sitting in the water. Quack, quack, quack."

There's a little green frog swimming in the water,
(*Place the frog on the lily pad.*)

A little green frog, doing what he oughta!
He jumped right off the lily pad,
That the little duck bit, and he said, "I'm glad
I'm a little green frog swimming in the water. Glub, glub, glub."

There's a little black bug floating in the water.
(*Place the bug on the water.*)

A little black bug, doing what he oughta!
He tickled the frog on the lily pad,
That the little duck bit, and he said, "I'm glad
I'm a little black bug floating on the water. Chirp, chirp, chirp."

There's a little red snake lying in the water,
(*Place the snake on the water.*)

A little red snake, doing what he oughta!
He frightened the duck and the frog so bad,
He ate the little bug, and he said, "I'm glad
I'm a little red snake lying in the water. Wriggle, wriggle, wriggle."
(*Remove all the animals.*)

Now there's nobody left sitting in the water,
Nobody left doing what he oughta!
There's nothing left but the lily pad.
(*Sing sadly.*)

The duck and the frog ran away. "I'm sad
'Cause there's nobody left sitting in the water.
Boo, hoo, hoo."

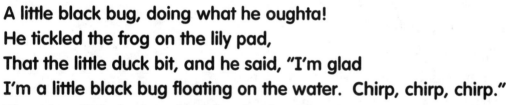

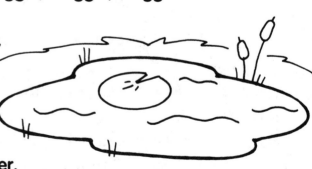

• •

Use the patterns on pages 71 and 72 for the characters in "Little White Duck."

• •

Patterns for Little White Duck

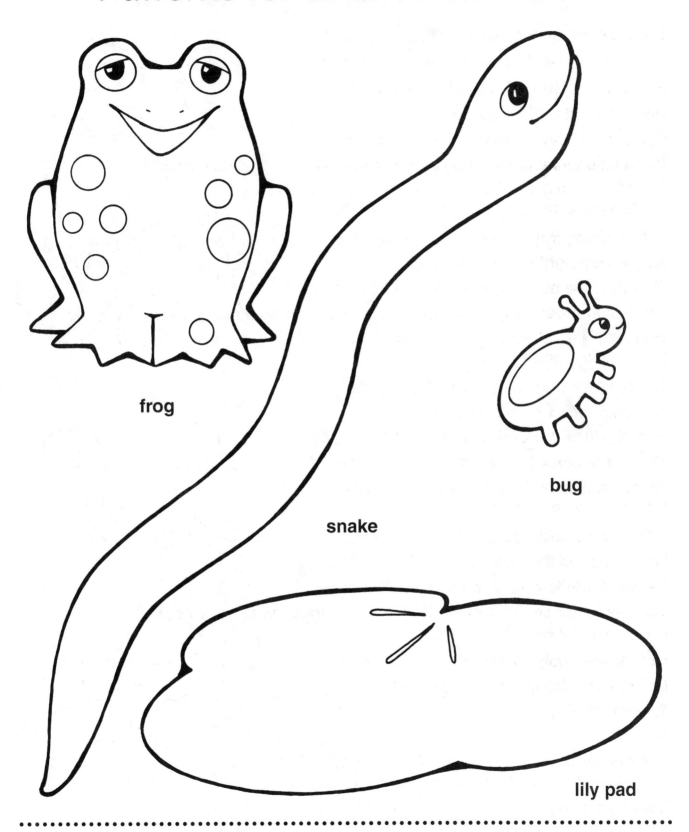

frog

snake

bug

lily pad

. . . .

1. Make one green frog.   3. Make one green lily pad.
2. Make one black bug.   4. Make one red snake.

. . . .

Patterns for Little White Duck *(cont.)*

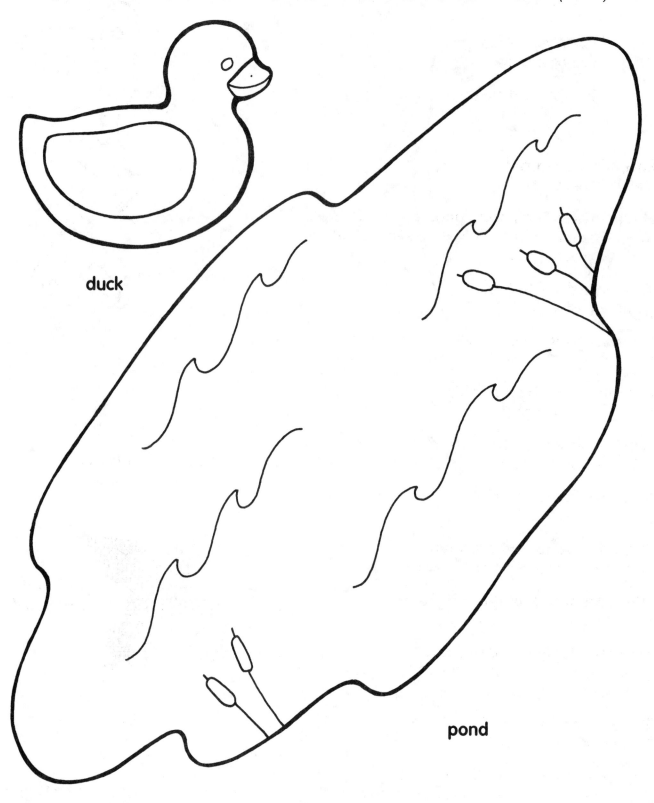

duck

pond

- -

1. Make one blue pond. Enlarge as much as possible.
2. Make one white duck. **Optional:** Add feathers and google eyes.

- -

Color Birds

Little bird, coat of blue,
(*Hold up the blue bird.*)

Tucked his tail and away he flew.
(*Move the blue bird up and down to simulate flying and tuck it behind your back.*)

Bird, bird, all in red,
(*Hold up the red bird.*)

Flapped his wings and shook his head.
(*Move the red bird up and down to simulate flying and shake your head.*)

Yellow bird in the top,
(*Hold up the yellow bird.*)

Here he goes, hop, hop, hop!
(*Move the yellow bird up and down to simulate hopping.*)

Orange bird, oh so bright,
(*Hold up the orange bird.*)

Spread his wings, flew out of sight.
(*Move the orange bird up and down to simulate flying and tuck it behind your back.*)

Bird, bird black, as night,
(*Hold up the black bird.*)

Turned around and then was white.
(*Turn the black bird over to show white side.*)

Whoever saw a purple bird?
(*Hold up the purple bird.*)

He cannot say a single word.
(*Move the purple bird up and down to simulate flying and tuck it behind your back.*)

I'm looking for a bird of green.
(*Hold up the green bird.*)

He is hidden and can't be seen.
(*Move the green bird up and down to simulate flying and tuck it behind your back. Repeat the poem and give each child a bird to help act out the poem.*)

• •

Use the bird pattern located on page 74.

• •

Patterns for Color Birds

1. Make eight stick puppet birds, one in each of the following colors—blue, red, yellow, orange, purple, green, black, and white.

2. Attach the wings to the back of the bird's body.

3. Use small, yellow diamond shapes for beaks and triangles for feet.

4. Glue the black bird to the cardboard on one side and the white bird to the cardboard on the other side. Place the end of the stick between the cardboard and the white felt.

Birds in a Tree

There was one little bird in one little tree.

(Arrange the tree and one bird on the flannelboard. Pass out the rest of the birds or place the birds at the bottom of the flannelboard.)

He was all alone, and he didn't want to be.

So he flew far away, over the sea,

And brought back a friend to live in the tree.

(Add a second bird to the tree.)

Two little birds in one little tree.

They were all alone, and they didn't want to be.

So they flew far away, over the sea,

And brought back a friend to live in the tree.

(Add a third bird to the tree.)
(Repeat with four, five, etc.)

Last verse:

There were ten little birds in one little tree.

"We're not alone any more."

Use the patterns for the tree and the bird on page 76.

Patterns for Birds in a Tree

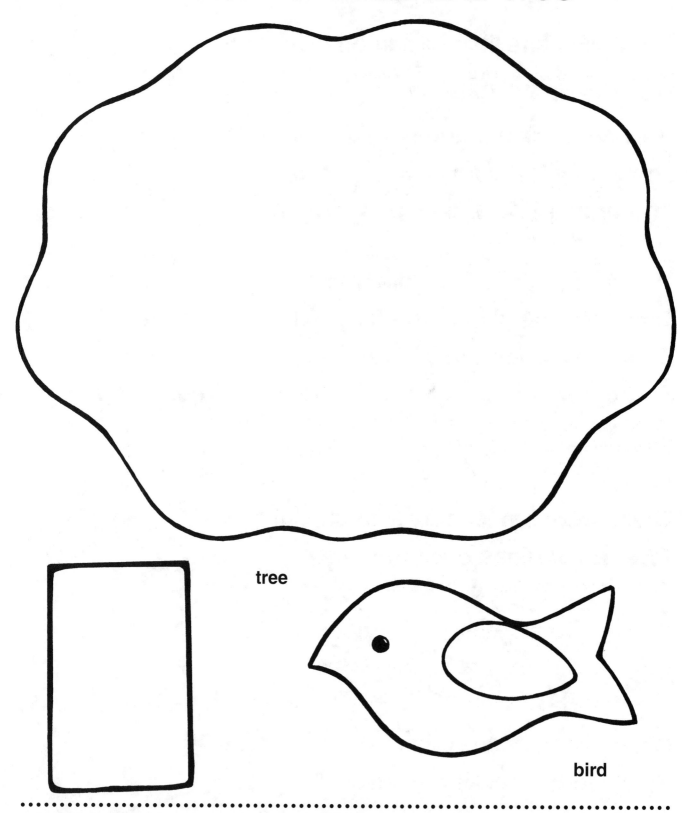

tree

bird

1. Attach the trunk to the back of the tree.
2. Make ten birds, one in each of the following colors—blue, red, yellow, orange, black, purple, green, pink, white, and brown.

Colors in Our World

Red, red, I see red.

It's an apple growing overhead.

(Place a red apple on the flannelboard.)

Yellow, yellow, I see yellow.

It's a banana, long and mellow.

(Place a yellow banana on the flannelboard.)

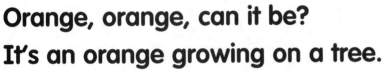

Orange, orange, can it be?

It's an orange growing on a tree.

(Place an orange on a tree on the flannelboard.)

Blue, blue, I see blue—

My kitten's eyes. She says,
"Meow, meow to you."

(Place a kitten on the flannelboard.)

Green, green, I see green.

From my garden, one string bean.

(Place a green string bean on the flannelboard.)

Purple, purple, what do I see?

Grapes on a vine, just for me!

(Place some purple grapes on the flannelboard.)

White, white, I see white—

Fluffy cloud, so soft and light.

(Place a white cloud on the flannelboard.)

· ·

Use the patterns for "Colors in Our World" located on pages 78 and 79.

· ·

Patterns for Colors in Our World

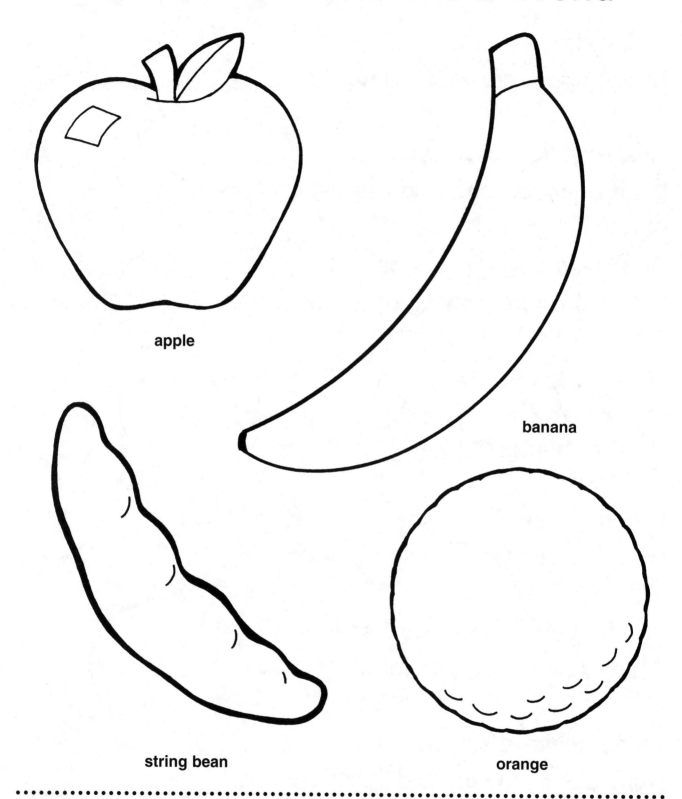

apple

banana

string bean

orange

1. Make one red apple.
2. Make one yellow banana.
3. Make one green string bean.

4. Make one tree. Use the pattern on page 76.
5. Make one orange.

Patterns for Colors in Our World *(cont.)*

kitten

grapes

cloud

1. Make a kitten with blue eyes.

2. Make a bunch of purple grapes.

3. Make a white cloud.

The Egg Who Couldn't Decide

Once upon a time, there was a little egg named Benedict, who didn't know what color he wanted to be.

(*Place a white egg on the flannelboard.*)

He said, "I've always liked the color of trees. Perhaps I should be green.

(*Place a green egg and a green tree on the flannelboard.*)

But then again, I like the color of carrots. Maybe I should be orange.

(*Place an orange egg and the carrots on the flannelboard.*)

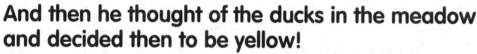

Of course, the color of water is pretty, too. I wonder how I'd look if I were blue,"

(*Place a blue egg and the water on the flannelboard.*)

And then he thought of the ducks in the meadow and decided then to be yellow!

(*Place a yellow egg and the duck on the flannelboard.*)

At that moment, a great big red fire truck drove by. Benedict said, "That's the color for me! I'll be red!"

(*Place a red egg and the fire truck on the flannelboard.*)

A moment later, when he saw a cow eating a bunch of grapes, he couldn't decide whether to be a purple egg or a brown egg.

(*Place a purple egg, a brown egg, the grapes, and the cow on the flannelboard.*)

"Oh, dear. Oh, dear," said Benedict. "I can't make up my mind. All those colors are so pretty." Just then, who should appear but his friend, the bunny.

(*Place a bunny on the flannelboard.*)

"Don't worry, Benedict," he said. "I know what to do!" And what he did made Benedict very happy. Do you know what the bunny did? He decorated Benedict in all his favorite colors.

(*Place a colorful egg on the flannelboard.*)

• •

Use the patterns for the "Egg Who Couldn't Decide" located on pages 72, 76, 81, and 82.

• •

Patterns for
The Egg Who Couldn't Decide

1. Make eight eggs in the following colors—white, green, orange, blue, yellow, red, purple, and brown.

2. Make a ninth egg. This egg can be multicolored or decorated with different colored clothing using the patterns above. (Use all of the colors to decorate this egg.)

3. Make orange carrots.

4. Make one yellow duck using the pattern on page 72.

Patterns for
The Egg Who Couldn't Decide *(cont.)*

bunny

cow

fire truck

1. Make a red fire truck, a brown cow, and a bunny.
2. Use the patterns on page 76 to make a green tree.
3. Use the pond pattern on page 72 to make blue water.
4. Use the pattern on page 79 to make purple grapes.

I Wore the Colors of the Rainbow

On Monday, I wore a red sweater that came up to my chin.

On Tuesday, I wore a pair of orange socks that made me grin.

On Wednesday, I wore a yellow shirt that looked like the sun.

On Thursday, I wore green pants. That was fun!

On Friday, I wore a blue scarf—the color was just right.

On Saturday, I wore a purple cap and my friend said, "You are out of sight!"

On Sunday . . . I wore all the colors of the rainbow.

Use the pattern to the right with the clothing on **page 84**.

Patterns for
I Wore the Colors of the Rainbow

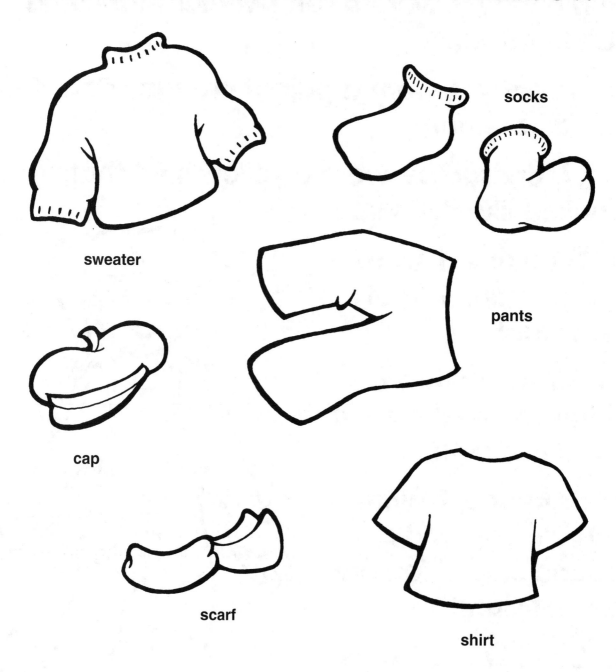

sweater

socks

pants

cap

scarf

shirt

1. Make a red sweater.
2. Make orange socks.
3. Make a yellow shirt.
4. Make green pants.
5. Make a blue scarf.
6. Make a purple cap.

Mr. Brown and Mr. Green

This is the story of two friends, Mr. Brown and Mr. Green. This is Mr. Brown and this is Mr. Green.

(Hold up fists, fingers bent around thumbs.)

One day Mr. Brown decided to visit his friend, Mr. Green. So he opened his door, popped out, and closed his door.

(Right hand clenched, open four fingers to the side, extend thumb up, close fingers.)

He went up the hill and down the hill and up the hill and down the hill until he came to Mr. Green's house.

(Thumb up, fingers bent, create up-and-down movements with arm.)

He knocked on the door. He knocked again.

(Knocking motion.)   *(Repeat knocking motion.)*

There was no answer. No one was home. So he went up the hill and down the hill and up the hill and down the hill until he got to his house.

(Thumb up, fingers bent, create up-and-down movements with arm.)

He opened the door, popped in, and closed the door.

(Hold fist up, extend four fingers, tuck thumb in, wrap fingers around thumb.)

The next day Mr. Green decided to visit his friend, Mr. Brown. So he opened his door, popped out, closed the door.

(Right hand clenched, open hand and extend four fingers, extend thumb up, close fingers.)

He went up the hill and down the hill and up the hill and down the hill until he came to Mr. Brown's house.

(Thumb up, fingers bent, make up-and-down movements with arm.)

He knocked on the door. He knocked again.

(Make knocking motion.)   *(Repeat knocking motion.)*

There was no answer. No one was home. So he went up the hill and down the hill and up the hill and down the hill until he got to his house. *(Repeat up-and-down movements.)*

Mr. Brown and Mr. Green (cont.)

The next day, at exactly the same time, Mr. Brown and Mr. Green decided to visit each other. They opened their doors, popped out, and closed the doors.

(Right hand and left hand are both clenched, open both hands and extend four fingers, extend thumbs up, close fingers.)

They went up the hill and down the hill, and suddenly, they met!

(Repeat motions, moving both hands at the same time.)

They talked and talked. They were so happy to see each other. Soon it was time to go home, so they said "Good-bye."

(Make fingers and thumbs go up and down, wave good-bye with each hand.)

And they each went up the hill and down the hill until they came to their own homes. Each one opened his door, popped in, and closed the door.

(Right hand clenched, open hand and extend four fingers, wrap fingers around thumb.)

And that is the story of the two friends, Mr. Brown and Mr. Green.

Use the patterns above for Mr. Brown and Mr. Green with patterns on page 87 to create a flannelboard story.

1. Cut out two bodies using skin-toned felt. Add faces to the bodies.

2. Make and attach a set of clothes in brown for Mr. Brown and another in green for Mr. Green.

Patterns for Mr. Brown and Mr. Green

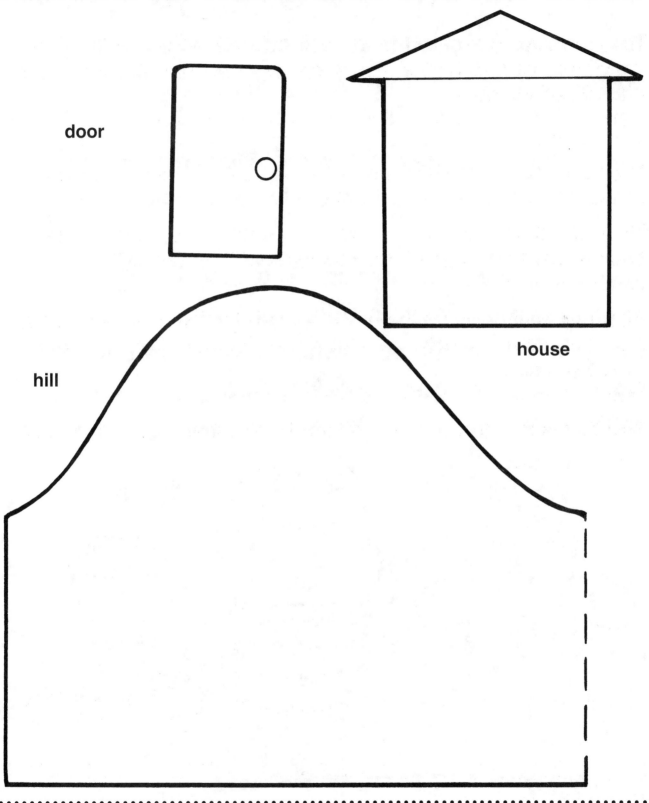

door

house

hill

1. Make two hills and connect them.
2. Make two houses with doors in different colors.

Green Speckled Frogs

Three green speckled frogs sat on a speckled log eating the most delicious bugs, yum, yum.

(Place three green frogs on log on flannelboard.)

One jumped into the pool, where it was nice and cool.
Now there are two green speckled frogs, glub, glub.

(Remove one frog.)

Two green speckled frogs sat on a speckled log eating the most delicious bugs, yum, yum.
One jumped into the pool, where it was nice and cool.
Now there is one green speckled frog, glub, glub.

(Remove one frog.)

• •

Patterns for the green frogs and the log are located on page 89.

• •

Patterns for Green Speckled Frogs

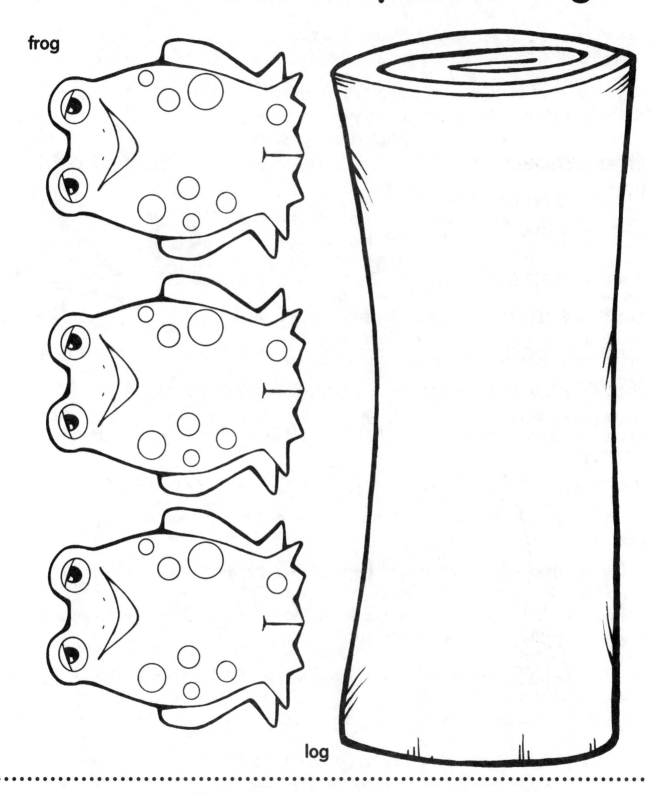

frog

log

....

1. Make three green speckled frogs and one log.
2. Use the pond from page 72 or use a large blue piece of fabric.

....

Zipper the Zebra

There once was a zebra who lived at the zoo.
(*Place the small, black and white zebra on the flannelboard.*)

The zebra had such a funny name. His friends called him Zipper! Wasn't that a silly name for a zebra to have? Boys and girls, can you say: "Zipper the Zebra?"
(*Repeat with children, "Zipper the Zebra?"*)

Do you know why they called him Zipper? Because he was very unhappy with his black and white suit. He was tired of wearing the same thing every day.

Do you wear the same clothes everyday? No, you don't! But Zipper had to wear the same black and white striped suit everyday. He wore it for his pajamas and school clothes....even for his play clothes.

He always wished that he might have a shiny zipper that would go from his head to his tail so that he could say "ZZZZZip" and take his suit right off. Can you say ZZZZZip?
(*Repeat "ZZZZZip" with children.*)

But have you ever seen an animal with a zipper? No, I never have either, so of course Zipper didn't have one!

One day when Zipper's mom was busy, Zipper decided to do something about his black and white suit. His little friend, Brown Bear, who painted pictures of animals to sell to the people who came to the zoo came over to see Zipper.
(*Place the brown bear on the flannelboard.*)

And quicker than you can say, "Zip, Zip, Zip," Brown Bear took out his red paint and painted Zipper bright red.
(*Exchange the red zebra for the striped zebra.*)

Let's see how he looks. He really looked funny. But Zipper thought he looked wonderful and he started off to show all of his friends who lived in the zoo. "Good morning, giraffe of the zoo. I've come over to play with you."
(*Place a giraffe on the flannelboard.*)

Zipper the Zebra *(cont.)*

But the giraffe just looked down at him, and said in very unfriendly voice: "Who are you? You do not belong in our zoo!" and poor Zipper said, "I am Zipper the Zebra, can't you see? I have a new suit to cover me."

Poor Zipper went to go look for someone else to play with.

"Good morning, Leo the Lion, I've come over to play with you."
(*Place a lion on the flannelboard.*)

But the lion just roared at him, and said in very unfriendly voice, "Who are you? You do not belong in our zoo!" and poor Zipper said, "I am Zipper the Zebra, can't you see? I have a new suit to cover me."

Poor Zipper went to go look for someone else to play with.

"Good morning, elephant of the zoo, I've come over to play with you."
(Place an elephant on the flannelboard.)

But the elephant just looked down at him, and said in very unfriendly voice: "Who are you? You do not belong in our zoo!" Poor Zipper said, "I am Zipper the Zebra, can't you see? I have a new suit to cover me."

But the elephant did not believe him. The elephant dipped his trunk into a tub of water and gave Zipper a great big squirt. As soon as the paint got wet it started to run.

"Zipper the Zebra, hee, hee, hee. You look more like a peppermint stick to me!"

Zipper had had enough and he ran home to his mother.
(Place the mother zebra back on the flannelboard.)

"Mother, it was not a good idea to want to change my suit, and I will never be unhappy with it again. I love it, because people don't know me without it. And I don't want to be called Zipper anymore because I do not want a zipper."

So she gave him a new name—"Zippy." Now everyone in the zoo calls him Zippy because he is such a happy zebra.

• •

Patterns for "Zipper the Zebra" are located on pages 92, 93, and 94.

1. Make three small zebras—one red, one red and white, and one black and white (Zipper).
2. Make one large black and white striped zebra (mother).
3. Make one brown bear.
4. Make one lion, one giraffe, and one elephant.

• •

Patterns for Zipper the Zebra

large zebra

brown bear

Patterns for Zipper the Zebra *(cont.)*

small zebra

giraffe

Patterns for Zipper the Zebra *(cont.)*

lion

elephant

94

I See Colors All Around Me

These are colors I can see,
(Put the color strip on the flannelboard.)

They are all around me.
(Motion all around the presentation area.)

White fluffy rabbits, gentle brown bats,
(Place the rabbit and the bat [upside down] on the board.)

Glowing orange pumpkins, furry black cats.
(Add the pumpkin and the cat to the flannelboard.)

Nice green grass, big yellow sun,
(Add the grass and the sun to the flannelboard.)

Bright blue sky, it is so much fun!
(Complete the scene with a strip of blue sky.)

white	brown	orange	black	green	yellow	blue

Use the patterns on page 96. Create a color strip showing all the colors mentioned in the poem. Make the strip using construction paper or fabric. Enlarge if possible.

Patterns for I See Colors
All Around Me

rabbit

bat

pumpkin

cat

1. Make one white rabbit.
2. Make one brown bat.
3. Make one orange pumpkin.
4. Make a black cat.

5. Use a strip of green felt for grass.
6. Cut out a 4" yellow circle for the sun.
7. Use a strip of blue fabric for the sky.